Woe to the Raging Storms

Cynthia Keffer

Copyright © Cynthia Keffer 2024

All rights reserved. No part of this book may be reproduced or transmitted in any form or by any means without written permission from the author.

Cynthia Keffer

cindykefferwork@gmail.com

828-407-7229

Dedication

This book is dedicated to my brother Allen, who was going through some trials in his life. The Lord laid such a burden on my heart for him and then gave me some wonderful thoughts to share with him and others. I pray it will encourage those who are facing trials in their own lives. I also pray that it encourages us to draw closer to the Lord in our daily walk with him.

About the Author

I am an insurance agent by trade. I am a believer and follower of Jesus Christ and have been for many years. I have struggled from time to time in my walk. There have been mountain tops, where I celebrated the victories, and there have been valleys low, where I have struggled. In those times of struggle, I have grown, but certainly not without growing pains. Those pains have taught me lessons, and honestly, I can say that I am thankful for them! I have found that this is true for many people. God always shows His faithfulness! I am sharing my testimony with the hope that my experiences in life might encourage others and help with their own valleys.

I love working with people! I love people! I have learned that no matter where we come from or how wealthy or poor we may be, we are all going to endure hard times in life! In those times, we all could use some encouragement. I hope the words of this book do just that: encourage you!

Sometimes, the clouds are blackened, the winds are howling, lightning crackles, and the thunder is loud and rolling. The seas are heightened with waves that seem as though they could swallow you up in a moment of time. With each wave that breaks seems that the storm grows more fierce. You can feel your heart beating within you. It seems to be the only noise other than the raging storm around you. Have you ever been in this storm before? Sometimes it seems frightening and sometimes even hopeless; I have certainly been there, but then……

I am taken to God's word. In Matthew 8:23, when Jesus and his disciples entered into a ship. There arose a great tempest in the sea, so much that the ship was being covered by the water. Jesus was sleeping during this storm. The disciples were afraid of the storm surrounding them. Why was not the master awakened? How could he possibly be sleeping at such a perilous time? They said to him, Lord save us, we perish. And he replied unto them, why are ye fearful, O ye of little faith? Are we too of little faith? Whether it is in the storms of life or the thunderstorms, do we also run and go unto the master crying out Oh Lord! Save us lest we perish?

Remember, no matter how black the storm clouds are or how high the waves get, all it takes is for the master to say Peace Be Still, and they have to obey. In the Bible, in the 26th verse of this passage, it reads: Then he arose and rebuked the winds and the sea, and there was a great calm (KJV). You see, he is in control of everything, even the storms.

In the book of Nahum, verse 1:3 says that the Lord has his way in the whirlwind and in the storm, and the clouds are the dust of his feet. This is a wonderful scripture. God is in control. No matter how bad the situation seems, there is nothing too great for him. He loves you; you are his child, and he desires to bring you comfort in the great storms of life. Remember, the next time it seems it is impossible to escape from the storms he said he would make an escape where there seemed to be none. He will speak to your storm and say Peace Be Still. He will not put on you more than you can bear.

Lord, when the waters are raging, and the waters are tossing me about, let me, oh Lord, find comfort in thy word. Let me know that those clouds in the sky are indeed the dust of your feet. Let me know that, as any parent, you desire that I am comforted by your presence and by your words. Thank you, Lord, for being my refuge, for rebuking the storms.

Never Alone

So many times, Oh Lord, we think that we must be in the church to be in your presence. That we have to be gathered with others before you will come and visit with us. We take that verse where two or three are gathered in your name there you will also be in the midst of them and think that is the only time you will be in our midst. Have we forgotten the times or events of our forefathers?

How you guided Moses by a cloud by day and a pillar of fire by night.

How you provided food for your servant Elijah during the drought in the wilderness and sent manna to him by a raven.

How you protected David when King Saul sought to kill him.

When the three Hebrew children were thrown into the furnace, you were right there with them.

Moses was chosen to lead the people of Israel out of bondage. He had the job of leadership. He had the responsibility of leading all of those people to safety. They were depending on Moses for everything, from guidance to food and water. They seemed to forget just what God had done in Egypt to get his children freed.

Elijah, during the drought, God told him to go to the Brook at Cherith, and he didn't tell him to take anyone with him. He went alone, and God provided food for him by a raven. Another time in God's word, we can also see that Elijah went to a cave alone, but God sent an angel to minister to him.

David, when King Saul turned on him, God was always with him. David had to totally depend on him for everything. God watched over David and kept him safe and even turned the tide and delivered Saul into his hands three different times.

The three Hebrew children, Meshac, Shadrack and Abendego, would not bow to a man-made God. Therefore, they were bound and thrown into the furnace, yet when the king looked into the furnace, he didn't just see the three Hebrews, but he saw another. The Bible said in the book of Daniel that the fourth man was walking about in the furnace and describes him as being like unto the Son of God.

You see, even in your times of trouble and when you feel alone, God is right there with you. Now, we may never face the fiery furnace or be the leader of many people, but we are still his children, and the Bible says he has no respect for persons. That means he loves one just as much as he loves the other. Sometimes, we need to be alone with God to listen to what he says to our hearts. He will build us up when we seem to be at our lowest.

Lord, though we be absent from others, let us, oh Lord, realize that we are never absent from thy presence. Let us be thankful to be gathered together to praise and worship you, for we know that you will be in our midst. However, Lord, we know that you are always with us and in our midst, whether we be alone or in a crowd.

Amen

Lo the Valleys

At times, Lord it seems the valley is so deep, long and lonesome. The mountains fail to reach my view. At times, oh Lord, it would seem as if I could never reach another mountain top. The road has become crooked and the road is rough. I think of others who might be going through this same valley or those who have been here before me. I think of God's word about the people in God's word that might have gone thru these valleys.

Even though their circumstances might have been different, I know that they still had to go through the low times in their walks with the Lord. Look at Daniel, who was thrown into the lions' den talk about a low valley. He was in a pit and still had hope in God. I think of Elijah, a great prophet of God who could pray and it wouldn't rain for three years. Yet he still had a valley that he had to face. In fact, he got so down that he hid himself in a cave, and God sent an angel of the Lord to minister to him. David wrote in the 23rd Psalm, yea I walk through the shadow of death, I will fear no evil for thou art with me, thy rod and thy staff they comfort me. Just when we think there is no hope or no end to the end of the valley, God will encourage us through his word. Psalm says that David encouraged himself in the Lord.

We must remember that it is in the valley where we do a lot of our growing, for the Lily of the Valley is there to see us through. He is blooming in the valley for us to behold His glory, his awe. There is none other like unto him. God on the mountain is still God in the valley. There is a scripture in Isaiah that says: Every mountain and hill shall be made low: and the crooked shall be made straight and the rough places plain. You will not always be in the valley, just as we will not always be on the mountain. When you can praise God in the valley just as well as on the mountaintop, you can say that you have grown.

Lord, the next time I am in that valley, remind me, oh lord where you have brought me from. Remind me, Lord, that you are that Lily in the valley and that flowing river in the desert. You are always with me, for you said that you would never leave me nor forsake me, but you would be with me unto the end of the world, for I know that you are the Rose of Sharon and the Alpha and Omega, the beginning and the end. You are the great I am. When you say it is time for me to leave that valley, then so be it; until then, let me thank you for the journey along the way and the growth that will come forth from the valley.

Amen

Last Thread of Hope

Ever since I can remember, it has been a struggle just to live. There have been times I have cried out for help just to find there was none to be found. I have been to Dr after Dr and even they say there is no help for me. I can't imagine what life would be like to be whole and not to be ill. Just once to be well, feel good like everyone else.

Maybe these are some of the thoughts that the woman in the Bible had, like the woman who had the issue of blood (blood disease, she was in much need of help). She looked everywhere for help and had spent all of her money yet no help. Have you ever been in a situation that seemed there was no help for you no matter what you tried? Your body is full of pain, yet you can't find any relief. It seems like you are hanging from your last thread of hope. Maybe it isn't a physical problem; maybe it is a drinking or a drug problem. Maybe it is not you maybe it is someone who is close to you or someone you know that has this problem. Either way, there is something that can be done; there is hope, a lifeline that you can throw to them.

You see, I know this first hand because I used to drink and I also had a drug problem. Many years ago, when I was a teenager, it started, if first started, with just a hit off of a cigarette, then a drink. Before I knew it, I was trying everything coming and going. I thought my life was awful, so I thought if I smoked weed or drank, it would make it better. Well, it didn't take long for the partying to take full control of my life.

You see, as a teenager, the devil makes things like that attractive for you. Don't believe it is a lie and an evil trick of his to get you started down that dark road. He wants you to think it is okay for you to do these things. Sometimes, you may think that there is no better way, but drugs or alcohol cannot give you real hope. It can only give false hope because it is not a fix to your problems. They may help you to forget them for a short period of time, but they don't make your problems go away in fact, they make the problems bigger.

There is hope, but it is found in Jesus, the redeemer of the world. Just as Jesus healed the woman with the issue of blood, he can do the same for you. He can take all of those things from you that have caused you pain, and he can fill you with unspeakable joy. He can give you peace that surpasses all understanding. God can help you through each trial and each situation. He may not deliver you from all of your troubles but he can help you through them. He will not leave you empty or feeling like you are missing something, for you will never feel better. He is there reaching out to you with a lifeline, wanting to save you or that loved one in this situation. If you see someone drowning, you do not just stand by and watch as they go under, but you try to save them. We do not have the power to save; only the Blood of Jesus can save. He said by his stripes we were healed. No matter what the sickness is, whether it is addiction or illness, he can make us whole. Just as he did the woman with the issue of blood, with just one touch of his garment, she was made whole.

Lord, we come to you in prayer asking you, Lord, to deliver whoever from these situations. Let them know that the drink the drugs will not help them; let them know that you have a better plan for their life. Lord, we ask you to save our lost loved ones and deliver those who have an addiction and think that they are hanging by their last thread of hope. We ask you to throw out the lifeline unto them. Lord, we ask that you heal that sick one, Lord, as you did the lady with the issue of blood. She just touched the hem of your garment sometimes Lord; that is all we need is to just touch the hem of your garment. Thank you, Lord, for delivering me from these things and just as you delivered me from them, I know, Lord, you can deliver others from the same things. Thank you, Lord, for reaching my way down to the depths of the gutter and saving my soul. I know that I no longer need drugs or drinks to make me happy. For your salvation has filled my emptiness and put a joy in my heart that is unexplainable. You are my help in the time of need. May others find such comfort in thee and such peace.

Amen

Solid Rock or Sinking Sand?

Is your house built on the rock or the sand? In the book of Matthew 7:24-27, it gives a parable about the two builders. As I read God's word and see what it states in this passage, I think about the church world. Verse 24 says: Therefore, whosoever heareth these sayings of mine, and doeth them, I will liken him unto a wise man who built his house upon a rock. This means it will be a strong and solid foundation. It will stand when others won't. You know, if you have ever walked on sand, it gives you your weight is put upon it. Yet when you walk upon a rock, it doesn't give at all. When the rains come, they wash the sand away. Yet the rock can stand the rain and not be moved. Sand will shift and be tossed to and fro with a small wind. A rock is a solid substance not easily blown or tossed to and fro by any little wind. There's a big difference between the two. This is how Jesus is comparing those who obey his words after hearing them and those who don't. In the 25th verse it says the rain come and floods came and the winds blew and beat upon that house (the house on the rock) and it fell not, for it was founded upon a rock. But if you go on to the 26th, it says and if everyone that heareth these sayings of mine and doeth them not, shall be likened unto a foolish man who built his house upon the sand; and the rain descended, and the floods came, and the winds blew and beat upon that house, and it fell, and great was the fall of it. You see if we build our faith on anything besides Jesus as our rock and our foundation, then we shall be like the builders who built their houses upon the sand. Therefore, we will not be able to stand.

We must learn God's word and be doers as well as hearers of the word. You can listen to God's word all day long, but you must also act upon it. We also need to know what God's word says and be able to discern what is of God and what is not. The Bible says to try the spirits among you to see if they be of God or not. We need to stick to sound doctrine and be rooted and grounded in the word. If not, we will be like the wells without water, clouds without rain, a house without a sound foundation. In the book of James 1:22; But be ye doers of the word and not hearers only, deceiving your own selves, for if any be a hearer of the word and not a doer, he is like unto a man beholding his natural face in a glass.

Lord, each day, let me read thy word and apply it to my life. Let it be my roadmap. May I forever stand on thee, for thou art the rock of my salvation. Let me forever seek to know thy word and hide it in my heart that I may not sin against thee. When the storms come, may I find comfort in knowing that my house is built upon the rock and will not fall? Though I am weak in the flesh, oh Lord, let my strength be found in thee.

Amen

Ankle Deep, Knee Deep or Too Deep

Have you ever asked yourself this question: Am I in too deep? When in all reality you're just wading and thinking all the time that you will just get wet up to your knees. Sometimes, we may have a fear of water, so we hesitate about getting wet at all. Some of us may feel that we might not be able to control the situation; therefore better just to be a sideline participant. Unfortunately, many times, our walk with God is just like that. We don't know what to expect; therefore, it is better not to venture any further.

If we just get our feet wet, we feel comfortable, for we are in a comfort zone. After a while, we may venture further, but only on our timetable and only on our terms. If we don't control the situation, it just doesn't sit well with us. This is the human way to be in control. This thinking puts God in a box.

Do you remember when you were little, and your parents taught you how to swim? At some point you had to trust them and let go and learn to paddle on your own. You had to trust that they would not let you drown. You knew that your parents would never let anything happen to you. They loved you, and they wanted what was best for you. Well, God is our Heavenly Father, and he cares for you. However, God wants to be in control. He wants us to turn our lives over to him completely and trust in him. He is trying to teach us how to swim. In order for us to learn, we must learn to let go and trust in the Father.

Maybe you haven't learned the basics of swimming yet because you are afraid to get wet. You must be willing to get wet in order to learn how to swim. Please come in the water is fine. Jesus is waiting to show you how to swim.

For those of you who have been swimming for a while, it is time to venture further out. There are no boundaries with God. Quit sitting around waiting for someone else to go out deeper first. Maybe God has called you for a certain work and you are fearful to answer that call. Maybe you are worried about what others will think of you. It could be that it would just be because it would require you to move from your comfort zone. Therefore, we quench the spirit. We ignore what God has laid on our hearts to do. If we ignore it long enough, it will go away…Maybe God will tell someone else to do the same thing. You are right. God will get someone else to do that task that he has asked you to do. He will also give that blessing to that obedient one who has done the work, the one who was willing to get out a little further with him. Many people look at Peter and say his faith was weak. Was it weak? I didn't read of anyone else who was willing to get out of the boat. He was willing to get out of his comfort zone and try something different. He was willing to trust in the Lord. Are you willing? Walk where he leads you to go. Swim in the deeper waters with the Lord; he will not let you drown.

In the book of Matthew, in chapter 5, Blessed are they which do hunger and thirst after righteousness for they shall be filled. Now, reading that tells me that if we hunger and thirst after God, we will be filled. James tells us in his writings that if we draw nigh to God, God will draw nigh to us. He will not leave us abandoned if we get out into the deeper waters. If we want a closer walk with God, then we will draw closer to him, and it is his promise to us that he will certainly draw closer to us.

If we have grown complacent and satisfied where we are with the Lord. My friend, that is a dangerous place to be. We must continually grow with God, or we wither away and die. Accepting Jesus as our personal Savior is not the first and last step. It is a necessary step but certainly not the last. That is only the beginning. If we are going to learn to get deeper in the relationship that we have with the Lord, we must put forth the effort. We need to read our Bibles daily. Pray daily; the Bible tells us to pray without ceasing. Go with a prayer in your heart.

Dear Lord,

I pray that you will help me to get out of my comfort zone. Let me be willing to go out a little further today than what I did yesterday. I desire that walk with you into deeper waters. I know, Lord, sometimes I must just let go and take off my wading shoes so I can get out further. I know that you are my lifejacket. Let all of us grow in you.

Amen

Bottle Fed or Table Food

You don't feed a newborn baby table food, and you wouldn't expect a grown-up to live on milk only. Therefore, when we are newborn Christians, we need to be fed milk. Just as a baby's diet increases with age, as we grow in the Lord, the meal gets more substantial each time. You see, you can only digest so much food at a time. If we eat too fast, we may be able to eat more, but we won't be able to retain all of it. If we eat slowly, we can digest it better. When we first learn of the Lord, we need to know the basics, what we must do to become his child.

The plan of salvation has been made so simple by God. People often try to complicate it by their rules or thoughts. There is only one way to the Father. Jesus said He was the way, the truth and the life, and no man cometh unto the Father but by him. He said if we would confess our sins, he is faithful to forgive us of our sins and cleanse us from all unrighteousness. He also said that whosoever called upon the name of the Lord shall be saved. You see, he made it quite simple, didn't he? There are no more blood sacrifices necessary. He was the ultimate sacrifice. He paid the debt he did not owe for you and me. We must believe that he died for us, that he was resurrected, and that we are all sinners and need him to cleanse us from our sins. That is what we hear when we are first saved. God is Love he loved us so much that He gave his only begotten son that whosoever believed in him should not perish but have everlasting life. You see, those are simple concepts that we can understand. We can understand that we love him because he first loved us. Most of the time, we understand that He is the one who changes our hearts; however, sometimes, we think that we have to clean up and then come to him. We will never be clean enough on our own to get to Heaven. It is only by the precious blood that Jesus shed on that cross that we are made righteous in his sight. The Bible says that our righteousness is as filthy rags in the sight of the Lord. Jesus is the only one who was perfect enough to pay for our sins because He knew no sin himself. He took the weight of the world's sin upon him so that we may have fellowship with the Father again.

When we first get saved, we read the Bible and its truths are revealed to us as milk. As we grow in the Lord and we pray and seek him, we find growth, not physical but spiritual. Our spiritual growth becomes apparent to others who are around us. Our speech changes, and our way of thinking changes because we take on the mind of Christ. We have begun to eat from the meat of the word. As we get older, we allow the Potter to put us on the Potter's wheel and let him have his way molding us. It is important to be attentive to the teaching and preaching. The Bible says in 1 Peter 2:2 as newborn babes, desire the sincere milk of the word, that ye may grow hereby you see if we don't get milk after that we are saved we won't grow.

Dear Lord:

Lord, I want to become more of a mature Christian. I am thankful for the milk of the word. I am thankful for the meat of the word, even though sometimes it steps on my toes. I pray as I grow each day that you would use the Word to nurture my soul and make it fat with your word. Make my heart more as yours, and let me illuminate your light each day. Lord enable me to become a mature person in you so that I may help others who are new in you to become more mature. For Lord, I know that you would not have us to stay as newborn babes in you. We must grow in you daily so that we may decrease in our physical man and increase in our spiritual man.

Amen

Casting a Shadow

There is a song about a shadow that I love dearly. The words sung by Ernie Dawson of Heirline really should tug at our heart's strings. The song, if you are not familiar with it, speaks of a little boy watching his Dad. Whether you are a parent or not, this song should speak to us. We all have someone watching us. It may be your co-workers, friends, parents, and or children, among others.

Little children mimic their parents. They pretend to work, talk on the phone, and even talk like their parents. That can be scary if we are not guarding our tongues as we should be at all times. In fact, most of the time, you can tell a lot about a child's home life if you just listen to them talk or watch their actions.

The same is true about a Christian. You can tell a lot about their walk with God with their speech and especially their actions. How people treat one another speaks volumes.

Unfortunately, sometimes, non-believers treat people better than those who profess to be followers of Christ.

The Bible even speaks of a cloud of witnesses that we are surrounded by (Hebrews 12:1). Jesus was our example and told us to follow him. He did the will of the Father, even when it wasn't politically correct. There are times in our Christian walk that we will not be politically correct. We will not be able to agree with the multitudes; our way of thinking will not be popular. Sometimes, our thinking may even seem to be irrational to others around us.

Let's look at a couple of places in the word of God. Acts 21(King James Version), when Paul was on notice that he would suffer and be bound, the people surrounding him tried to talk him out of going. In Matthew 16 (King James Version), Jesus is telling his disciples about the suffering he is going to have to endure, and Peter rebukes him. Wow! People even did the same to Jesus. Jesus was speaking something that was not popular; it was not a feel-good message, and what did he get? Rebuke.

Here are two examples taken right from the Holy Bible that show that even though it was not rational with man's thinking, God had a plan. These two passages show us that Jesus and Paul both followed the will of the Father. Though it may not have been the popular way to go or the logical it was the way of the Father.

Even those close to these two, Jesus and Paul, tried to talk them out of doing what they had planned. Surely, there must have been a different way through Peter and the believers crying over Paul's departure. However, they both, with determination, kept steadfast in their journey because they knew it was the will of the Father. Now, ladies, do not think that you are left out of this group. Remember Mary, chosen vessel of God, yet her path would lead her down a road of judgement.

People thought she had been impure and what a terrible shadow she would be casting upon her family. Just the thought of a pregnancy out of wedlock, today it is not a big deal in our society, but it once was not the standard. Telling everyone that God had spoken to her and that the events that would take place after would be all part of God's plan. Well, can you imagine telling your parents such a thing? Can you imagine their reaction to Mary? Yet, here is this young virgin who is fixing to carry the Son of God. This was all part of God's plans. However, just because something is God's plan does not mean that it will set well with mankind. We as Christians must remember that man's ways are not God's, nor are man's thoughts God's. However, if we are going to allow our shadows something that we would want our children to follow in, to mimic we must be willing to go against the popular, against the status quo. We must be willing to be different, set apart, a peculiar people. How is your shadow casting today? Is it what you want your children to grow up to be? Do you want to be remembered for the life you led for Jesus or the way you lived to please man?

Dear Lord,

As you lived a life after the Father, let my heart's desire be the same. Let me make sure that I am lining up with the Word of God. Let me be sensitive to the Spirit of God. Let me stand for what is Right instead of whatever is popular. Let my life be a legacy that is note worthy of you. Let my heart be right, my mind aligned, and my spirit strong to stand where I need to stand.

Amen

Becoming more like Jesus

Compassionate, loving, a friend to the poor, merciful, and forgiving, oh what a list of qualities to have within you. Loving people who hate you, blessing those which curse you, praying for those who use you, does that sound like you? That is the life Jesus led and lived. It is also the commandment He has given to us to fulfil as well.

He was moved with compassion in Matthew 14:14 when he seen the great multitude and healed their sick. This compassion came even though he had just learned of John the Baptist's beheading. Even though he had got on a ship and went into a desert place, people heard about it and followed him. He put aside his personal hurt and sorrow and took compassion upon the crowds. Oh, my goodness, could we put our losses aside so quickly to address the current moment and need? Could we be so selfless to think of others instead of our sorrow at that very moment?

Jesus was able to do so and remember He is our example. Surely, we all mourn we all get upset at times. We all even feel sorry for ourselves from time to time. However, if we could only focus on the current surroundings and needs of others, then we would have less time to focus on our sorrows and sadness. At that very moment, Jesus healed their sick. Wow, he gave healing to those who were sick. Perhaps in those sick, he may have given new hope to someone who had given up on ever being well.

He was loving when he was hated. Even more, he was loving to the very ones who hated him. He prayed for their forgiveness; how much more love can a person show? Could we do the same? Imagine someone pounding a nail in your foot, shoving a spear in your side, your body in pain from the nails in your hands or the crown of thorns around your head. What about the mental anguish? Where were all those who so highly esteemed him? He had a multitude of followers just a little while ago; where were they all now? Alone, he was on that cross, not a friend in sight. Yet even in all that, what were his thoughts? Father, into thy hands, I commend my spirit. His words were not anything of revenge, hate, bitterness, or sorrow. He did not cry out. Father got them. Father, forgive them, is what he said. To be like Jesus.

Putting another and all above our mental and physical needs. Letting the love of Jesus shine through when we have been hurt. Oh, what love! What compassion!

Jesus was always putting others before himself. He didn't demand a home to lay his head on. He didn't demand or even state that he deserved such things as fine clothing, the best meal, the best place to dwell, or even servants. No, not Jesus.

Lord, each day, people say things to one another that are unkind and hurtful. People knowingly and purposely hurt one another, yet ye taught us that we could overcome these actions with love. Thank you for showing us such compassion and love. May each of our hearts be full of the same. May we show grace even when it is not deserved. May we show love in times of pain. Let our lips not be quick to throw back hurt or resent but to slowly meditate upon thee, oh Lord. May our speech may be representative of the love that you have for all people.

Amen

Missed Opportunities

Have you ever thought about missed opportunities in your life? Maybe it was a job, a trip, or a relationship. Have you ever said to your self what if? Where would I be right now if I had taken that opportunity? What would I be doing? How would my life be different? Maybe you have even had regrets about not taking the opportunities that have passed you by….

In the Bible, we are told about a couple of passed-up opportunities. Here is a man who is told that he could have eternal life forever, never need for nothing again. Yet he is so wrapped up in material things he cannot see the big picture. Many times, we get short-sighted and only see what is in front of us instead of what could be. The things of this world can weigh us down, and we forget that we are strangers in a land that is not our eternal home.

Sure, we all need money to live. We all have obligations of sorts that have to be fulfilled. However, how many of those obligations or duties satisfy the soul? Years ago, someone said to me we work to live, and we don't live to work. I meditated on that saying and thought, how many of us really work to live or are driven by work and that has become our life? This gentleman in the Bible who had his barns full and was ready to build more seems to be a little of the latter. Luke 12:15-21the man was being given a warning not to covet. Life is not about what possessions you can have or obtain. Life is more than new cars, fancy homes, or other belongings. For these things do not last. Possessions may make you feel good for a season, and food fills your body for a span, but

only Jesus, being the bread of life, will fill you with a satisfaction that cannot be filled any other way. This man was not thinking spiritually, only physically. He was wrapped up in the now rather than in the future. Does any of this strike home with you? Are we so caught up in trying to make it in this world that we neglect our spiritual home?

Sometimes, we need to stop worrying about how we will pay for this or that and focus more on the one thing that has already been purchased for us. Life, our lives are not our own. We have been purchased with a price. The price of the precious blood of Jesus. Jesus tells his disciples not to take no thought for our lives, or what we shall eat, or what we shall wear. Jesus states in Luke 12:23 that life is more than meat, and the body more than raiment.

We have to live but live unto Christ and not the world. Don't miss any opportunity given to you by the Lord. These opportunities can be giving an encouraging word, praying for someone, helping someone in need, or giving a person life through the Word of God. We all have opportunities each day given to us. Please just remember that no matter what opportunity is given, make sure that your emphasis is on the ones that will last for eternity and not short-lived.

Lord, may I live each day as if it were my last. May my tongue be guarded and directed by you. Order my steps oh Lord, in the direction you would have me to take. Open the doors you would have me to travel through and close those you would not. Lord, let me take every opportunity that you afford me and let me not pass them by. For it is the opportunity, Lord, that someone took that allows me to know you today. Let my life be a light so others may see you when they look at me. Thank you for every opportunity you give us each and every day.

Amen.

www.ingramcontent.com/pod-product-compliance
Lightning Source LLC
LaVergne TN
LVHW061043070526
838201LV00073B/5158